Debbi + Oz Crosby
STAG #2

TOM TILL
UTAH
MAGNIFICENT WILDERNESS

PHOTOGRAPHY BY TOM TILL

WESTCLIFFE PUBLISHERS, INC. ENGLEWOOD, COLORADO

CONTENTS

International Standard Book Number:	*ISBN 0-942394-60-7*
Library of Congress Catalogue Card Number:	*87-051500*
Copyright, Photographs and Text:	*Tom Till, 1989*
Editor:	*John Fielder*
Assistant Editor:	*Margaret Terrell Morse*
Production Manager:	*Mary Jo Lawrence*
Typographer:	*Dianne J. Borneman*
Printed in Korea by:	*Sung In Printing Co., Ltd., Seoul*
Published by:	*Westcliffe Publishers, Inc.*
	2650 South Zuni Street
	Englewood, Colorado 80110

Bibliography

1. Stegner, Wallace, *Mormon Country*. New York: Bonanza Books, Division of Crown Publishers, Inc., MCMXLII. Reprinted by permission of the author.
2. Stegner, Wallace, *One Way to Spell Man*. New York: Doubleday & Company, Inc., 1982. Reprinted by permission of the publisher.
3. Stegner, Wallace, *The Sound of Mountain Water*. New York: E.P. Dutton, A Dutton Paperback, 1980. Reprinted by permission of the publisher.

First Frontispiece: *Paintbrush wildflowers bloom on the slopes of Albion Basin, Wasatch National Forest*

Second Frontispiece: *Cave shelters an Anasazi Indian ruin, Canyonlands National Park*

Third Frontispiece: *Interplay of shadow and light in Slickhorn Canyon along the San Juan River, Glen Canyon National Recreation Area*

Title Page: *Bighorn sheep pictograph in Salt Creek Canyon, Canyonlands National Park*

Right: *Oak and maples awash with fall color in Spanish Fork Canyon, Uinta National Forest*

FOREWORD

In his preface to this stunning book, Tom Till confesses that he was seduced. What first brought him to Utah — bizarre scenery — became an addiction, a passion, an exploration, a career, a life. He reversed the usual American habit of remodeling Eden with blasting powder and bulldozers, and let Eden remodel him. He won or conquered no wilderness; he submitted to it. Like Everett Ruess, the romantic young wanderer who vanished from a gulch off the Escalante in 1934, and like Edward Abbey, whose legacy some Utahns *wished* would vanish, Till has melted into the country, has surrendered his senses to desert forms and colors and his consciousness to space, solitude and silence.

That sounds mystical. In Utah, it is almost commonplace. No region in America, and so far as I know in the world, has a comparable power to evoke from human beings such responses of surprise, delight and, above all, awe. On people of sensibility — and there are surprising numbers of them — this country imposes itself in quasi-religious terms: Earth not as fertile mother, but as remote, austere, impersonal Power, humbling to the human ego. Time here is geological; the sky breathes the cold wind of space.

I know how this country feels to Tom Till because I know how it has felt to me ever since I began to know it in the early 1920s. That feeling comes back as fresh as new while I turn these pages. Because I feel protective about the Utah landscape and have been resisting the forces that would exploit it for boom-and-bust dollars, one of the happiest perceptions I get from Till's book is that there is still so much for him to see and revere, and for us to try to save.

Even though I have grown too old for hiking hard trails or climbing cliffs or sleeping on rockpiles and in inner spring washes, these superb pictures permit me a plausible and persuasive return. They remind me what a tremendous thing it once was to sit on the 11,600-foot rim of the Aquarius Plateau and look down across the Waterpocket Fold, toward and beyond the gray, snow-patched bubbles of the Henry Mountains, across the glowing red desert that I knew dropped off at the Orange Cliffs into what is now Canyonlands National Park, and beyond those seen or sensed rims to the high snowfields of the La Sals, and still beyond to where the faint tracery of the La Plata Mountains, 200 miles away in Colorado, haunted the horizon. Thanks to the Four Corners and Page power plants, that view has been shortened by at least 50 miles, but it *was* there and these photographs revive it.

There is more to this landscape than sheer space. There is sanctuary, too, cover, shelter that is essential in a stone desert close to the stars. Take your eye off the distances and you see it everywhere on the Colorado Plateau, from Comb Wash to the Hurricane Cliffs, from Bryce and Cedar Breaks to the Kanab Desert. Here, there are places to hide: alcoves, washes, grottoes, box canyons, slot canyons, caves, domed amphitheaters, overhangs. Many of these have seeps, springs, plunge pools; in many of them are the mortared houses and storage cisterns of the Anasazi who once found a home here.

Till's visuals have no accompanying audios, but as I study them I think I hear the drip and plash of secret water, the rattle of cottonwood leaves, the sweet falling song of canyon wrens; and if I imagine myself walking out at twilight to contemplate evening from the canyon rim, in a moment of attention that is like prayer, I hear the other, surrounding, abiding sound: the roar of utter silence, the noiseless *whoosh* of earth hurtling through space.

The Colorado Plateau, colorful and awesome as it is, is not all of it. In the Wasatch Mountains at whose feet most of Utah lives, there are patches of reserved alpine wilderness; in the Uintas there is a great one. In those areas and on the high plateaus of central Utah, the ground in July is solid flowers. And out in the western

Swirling runoff after an August flash flood,
Colorado River

desert, lifting out of playas and the temporary overflow of Great Salt Lake, is country even less known and visited than the alpine or slickrock wildernesses. The House Range, the Stansburys, the Wah Wahs and other Great Basin mountains contain secret beauty spots without a human footprint in them, streams and lakes and pockets of forest that only a few locals know.

In the Great Basin, plant life begins at the very edges of the salt flats and changes through many zones of altitude — saltbush to creosote bush to big sagebrush to piñon and juniper to ponderosa pine, and in the high, snowy canyons, more ancient than Roman ruins, the bristlecones that are the next-to-oldest living things on earth. Animal life changes along with the plant life. In all the world there is no other such place for the study of life's adaptations, for these plants and animals have been evolving without interruption since the Pleistocene epoch a million years ago.

Without interruption except by man. Mineral and oil exploration, chaining of piñon and juniper for "range improvement," the introduction of Russian thistle, cheatgrass and other exotic weeds, have already threatened large areas of both the western deserts and the Colorado Plateau. Look at these pictures of Tom Till's and see if you want the places he has found and captured on film to be defaced, battered, torn up and turned upside down for the profit of a few exploiters, or if you don't agree they should be put into the wilderness system and left as God made them.

— WALLACE STEGNER

Editor's Introduction

Forty years ago Wallace Stegner cut his environmental teeth during a fight to protect the Green River from damming as it flowed through Dinosaur National Monument in northeastern Utah. A book he edited and helped write — *This is Dinosaur* — was part of a groundswell that turned the tide of public and congressional opinion, and the Green River still flows free today. Thus lured from behind his typewriter and out into the activism spotlight by his love for Utah's rugged plateau and canyon country, Stegner has been a vital force in this country's environmental movement ever since.

Stegner's stock-in-trade remains his trusty Remington typewriter; over the years he has published 27 books as well as countless stories, articles, essays and reviews. A doctor of literature for more than 50 years, he founded the Stanford Writing Program in 1946, which he then directed for 25 years. It's not surprising the man has been called "a walking tower of American letters," for he has won both a Pulitzer Prize and a National Book Award for his fiction.

Even 40 years ago when the waters of the Green River were his focus, Stegner was no stranger to Utah. While studying and later teaching at the University of Utah, he had learned to love the state's rugged wilderness, an appreciation he has carried with him ever since. In the early 1960s, as a consultant to then-Secretary of the Interior Stewart Udall, Stegner toured the area around Capitol Reef National Monument, then recommended the monument be given national park status. Eventually his opinion was heard.

On the pages of this book Wallace Stegner is also heard, for he has hiked the mountains and canyons where Tom Till has exposed his film. Together, through words and images, Stegner and Till tell the largely unseen story of the wild side of Utah.

— Margaret Terrell Morse

Sunset illuminates tumbleweed, Great Salt Lake

PREFACE

I was seduced. While my college roommates were busily preparing for their lives as computer experts and landscape architects, I was plodding through my studies at a large midwestern university and obsessively scouring the maps of Canyonlands, Arches and Zion national parks that covered my walls. After a few visits to Utah as a child and later as a college student on semester breaks, I found myself falling deeply in love with the light, the mystery and the loneliness of southern Utah.

For many of my friends it was the same. Somehow we had been picked by the canyon country, and even though we were not aware of the immensity and complexity of the land that had cast its spell upon us, we began exploring its secrets. We were always amazed that it was wilder, bigger, more dangerous and more beautiful than we could have imagined.

The maps told us a few things, but they were just rudimentary guides. Beyond the maps were deep, narrow canyons with frigid pools of water untouched by sunlight even in June. We found Anasazi Indian ruins and pictographs like the Sky Faces, ghostly white visages painted high above a canyon at the top of a narrow sandstone fin. On the craggy summit of Mount Ellsworth in the Little Rockies Wilderness Study Area, we looked out in wonder over the familiar canyons and mesas unfolding in a full circle panorama.

About 10 years ago I began to take along a camera. One of my initial motivations was that I was often in country that had not, amazingly, been photographed much before. Desolation Canyon, for example, a gorge as deep as the Grand Canyon but located in central Utah, is little known outside the state. So far its buttressed walls and stone arches thousands of feet above the Green River have, unfortunately, escaped permanent protection as wilderness. My family and I traveled through this canyon recently on a series of perfect October days. It was a special river journey warmed by the waning autumn sun and touched by golden cottonwoods around every bend. We saw no one in five days except a cowboy who waved wanly to us from the far shore.

Another river canyon, Westwater Canyon near Moab, is unparalleled for scenic beauty and river running excitement. It is also so little known that photo editors refused to believe that an image I made several years ago of its river-sculpted Precambrian rock was not the Inner Gorge of the Grand Canyon. After the photograph appeared on the cover of a national magazine, a prominent environmentalist made speeches maintaining it was taken in Arizona, not Utah. Even those who should know better sometimes haven't fathomed the variety and extent of the Utah wilderness.

This wilderness is also an integral part of Utah's famous national parks and monuments. Outside the bustling and sometimes urban atmosphere of Zion Canyon, narrow slot canyons sinuously make their way through Navajo sandstone toward the Virgin River. One late October day, Bruce Hucko, Glen Lathrop and I rappelled our way down one of these nameless passages with all our photographic equipment, including 4x5 cameras and a large wooden tripod.

At first the going was easy and we were sure we would make our destination, the Zion Narrows, in a matter of hours. Our progress was eventually stymied, however, by a huge lake or reservoir formed when a rockfall ahead dammed the canyon below us. With no jumars to climb out the way we had come, we were committed to continuing through the icy lake. We spent precious time constructing a makeshift raft to carry the camera gear, then began the long swim to the last available sunlight across the lake. There, shivering and hypothermic, we realized our time was running out. We had now reached a section where the walls stood only a few feet apart and icy water rushed on all sides of us. At one point, my tripod slid under the surface of a deep, frigid pool. After several dives in his wet suit, Glen came up with it and we continued. As darkness approached we were only a few hundred yards from the narrows.

Sunset paints Fiery Furnace, an Entrada sandstone formation, Arches National Park

But more obstacles confronted us. A huge pine had fallen in the narrow corridor, allowing passage over a 50-foot drop-off only on its wet, mossy back. With courage derived from large amounts of adrenaline and the thought that we were slowly succumbing to hypothermia, we rushed across the log with ease. There, in darkness, was our final rappel, through a cascading waterfall that dropped more than 100 feet into the black Virgin River narrows below. One by one we descended to safety, feeling our way slowly along the slippery rocks, drenched continually by the falls. In a half hour, we were back to the paved narrows trail. No pavement had ever looked so good.

Appreciation for the Utah red rock country has flourished in recent years, but the vast Great Basin deserts have not received as much respect. My hope is that Utahns and others will become aware of the beauty and wilderness values of areas like the House Range near Delta. On its dizzying limestone cliffs bristlecone pines frame emerald Sevier Lake far below. Such otherworldly landscapes are common in the seldom-visited mountains and playas near the Nevada border.

Nothing, however, prepared me for the Bonneville Salt Flats, perhaps the easiest place in Utah to produce interesting photos. I once watched from the summit of the Silver Island Mountains as peak shadows stretched for dozens of miles across the ivory expanses of the flats. In September I saw the limitless salt flats transformed overnight by rains into a huge, shallow inland sea.

Near the summit of a remote Great Basin range, after an all-day hike, I photographed Utah's largest cave opening. Its huge arcing dome of orange limestone, hundreds of feet high and wide, framed range after range marching into Nevada. No winds could reach the back recesses of the grand opening to remove footprints in the fine limestone dust of the cave, yet we found no sign of others ever having been inside.

The Wasatch and Uinta ranges are the home of some of Utah's finest designated alpine wilderness. In northern Utah's mountains I have often been an observer of the great storms that furiously attack these ranges. I once cowered in my tent during a violent summer storm in the Uintas as lodgepole pines snapped and fell all around me. The sickening cracks and inevitable crashes of the great trees were a frightening reminder of nature's power over not only me, but the seemingly unchanging mountains. At other times I have marveled at the Wasatch mountains' luxurious wildflowers and their fall color displays that rival any of New England.

Although public opinion polls continually show most Utahns favor wilderness protection of more areas in the state, Utah has lagged behind other western states in wilderness designation. The photographs captioned "Wilderness Study Area" in this book were taken in areas identified as offering "outstanding opportunities for solitude," in other words, wilderness, by the Bureau of Land Management, which oversees 22 million acres in Utah.

I have photographed, hiked and boated in many of these areas, and their beauty and wilderness potential are the equal of anything on display in our magnificent parks. The Utah Wilderness Coalition Proposal for preserving the land, wildlife, rivers and forests of 5.1 million BLM acres deserves the support of everyone, nationwide, who loves the slickrock and the stillness, the great rapids and the ghostly bristlecones, the ancient ruins and the rushing trout streams. It's all here. Take a look.

— TOM TILL

For Marcy

Ice patterns on the Colorado River,
Canyonlands National Park

COLOR

The great photographer Eliot Porter once complained that some who saw his photos of Utah were skeptical about the colors. They were certain no such colors could exist in reality. Those who have spent much time in our state know that the purity of the light, the topography and the striking hues of the landscape conspire to produce vibrant and wonderfully saturated color. I enjoy photographing these intensely colorful scenes, not to shock or impress, but to revel in the interaction of light, rock, sky, water and film. I also find it just as exciting to seek out subtle colors, like the pale browns of a hoary juniper trunk, the pastels of rocks on the Great Salt Lake shore or the monochromatically gray bentonite hills near Capitol Reef.

Mule's ears wildflowers bloom at sunset, Fisher Towers

Overleaf: *Reeds rise up in Whirlpool Canyon, Dinosaur National Monument*

First rays of dawn on wet salt formations,
Bonneville Salt Flats

Paintbrush wildflowers blanket Albion Basin,
Wasatch National Forest

"The West's ultimate unity is its aridity. In other ways it has
a bewildering variety. Its life zones go all the way from arctic
to sub-tropical, from reindeer moss to cactus, from mountain
goat to horned toad. Its range of temperatures is as wide as
its range of precipitation . . . .

Afternoon light on Double Arch Alcove, Zion National Park

Golden buckwheat glows on an August afternoon, Zion National Park.

Overleaf: *Autumn palette below Mount Timpanogos, Alpine Loop*

. . . It runs through twelve degrees of latitude and nearly three miles of altitude. It is shortgrass plains, alkali flats, creosote-bush deserts, irrigated alluvial valleys, sub-arctic fir forests, bare sun-smitten stone."

Reflections of Hayden Peak in a small alpine pond,
High Uintas Wilderness

Autumn-painted cottonwood in Courthouse Wash,
Arches National Park

". . . the alpine and forest wildernesses are obviously the
most important, both as genetic banks and as beauty spots.
But for the spiritual renewal, the recognition of identity, the
birth of awe, other kinds will serve every bit as well."

The Colorado River reflects sandstone at sunset,
near Moab

Spring blossoms of claret cup cactus,
Arches National Park

". . . the western half of the country inherits the memory
and assumes the dream. It is younger and less altered; its
vast open spaces create the illusion of a continuing
opportunity that its prevailing aridity prohibits."

Peaks of the Wasatch Range seen from Mount Timpanogos, Mount Timpanogos Wilderness

Wintery sunset lights Fiery Furnace, Arches National Park

". . . the dusk come[s] on, the earth darkening before the sky, as if a smoke came up out of the valley and blotted out the shadowed ledges, merged black juniper and red rock. . . . "

FORM

Any form imaginable, and some that are not, can be found in the surrealistic plateau landscape of southern Utah. At Bryce Canyon alone, an infinity of rock spires and hoodoos has been created by the chance interaction of water, sandstone and time. Elsewhere in the canyons, desert varnish — ebony streaking on the sandstone cliffs — creates tapestries and patterns on a massive scale. The great uplifts — the San Rafael Swell, the Cockscomb, the Monument Upwarp — all challenge the desert sky with jagged fierceness. In northern Utah, the forms of the great peaks — Timpanogos, Hayden, Olympus — and the deep canyons dominate the landscape. The beauty of a claret cup cactus or the repetitive patterns of daisies show that form is also an essential element of the small scenes beneath our feet.

Pine reaches for the afternoon sun,
Bryce Canyon National Park

Overleaf: *Mirror Lake at dawn,*
High Uintas Wilderness

Looking through North Window at Turret Arch,
Arches National Park

Striped sandstone at Waterpocket Fold,
Capitol Reef National Park

"The horizon reels with surrealist forms, dark red at the
base, gray from there to rimrock, the profiles rigid and
angular and carved, as different as possible from the Navajo's
filigreed, ripple-marked sandstone."

Ice buildup at sunset, Bear Lake

Morning light on lava pebbles,
Snow Canyon State Park

Overleaf: Mesa Arch soars on Island in the Sky,
Canyonlands National Park

" . . . the eye is not merely invited but compelled to notice
the large things. . . . there is nothing visible but the torn
and slashed and windworn beauty of absolute wasteland.
And the beauty is death. Where the grass and trees and
bushes are stripped off and the world laid naked you can
see the globe being torn down and rebuilt."

The face of Notch Peak looms above the Great Basin
area, House Range Wilderness Study Area

Rime-covered trees in Big Cottonwood Canyon,
Wasatch National Forest

"The outermost line of plateaus forms . . . the boundary of
the Great Basin, a region of jagged and crazy ranges rising
from irreclaimable desert."

Sandstone hoodoos under an August sun,
Goblin Valley State Park

Frozen seeps, Negro Bill Canyon
Wilderness Study Area

". . . [the] country reveals itself as a bare-stone, salmon-pink
tableland whose surface is a chaos of domes, knobs, beehives,
baldheads, hollows, and potholes, dissected by the deep
corkscrew channels of streams."

Battered door of a bootlegger cabin,
Desolation Canyon Wilderness Study Area

Stream washes over limestone ledges,
Gold Bar Canyon

"It is a lovely and terrible wilderness . . . harshly and
beautifully colored, broken and worn until its bones are
exposed, . . . and in hidden corners and pockets under its
cliffs the sudden poetry of springs. . . ."

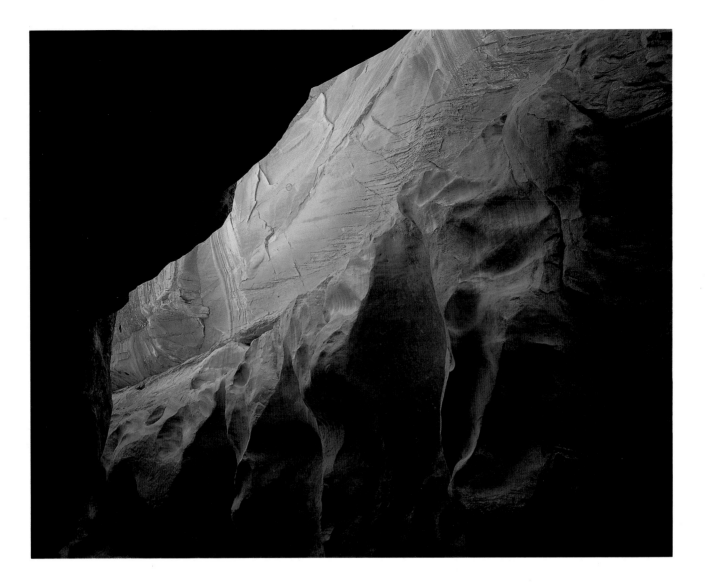

Water-sculpted sandstone inside a slot canyon,
White Canyon

Morning light on an ancient juniper trunk in the
House Range, Howell Peak Wilderness Study Area

" . . . a man can walk into a canyon . . . and be face to face
with two or three petrified minutes of eternity. That is worse,
in some ways, than facing eternity itself, because eternity is
a shadow without substance. Here is the residue of a few
moments, geologically speaking. "

MOMENT

Over the years I've come to expect two kinds of landscape photographs to come my way. In one kind of photograph, I carefully plan to be at a locale at a certain season and certain time of day. This method produces excellent results but may require hours, days or even months of patient waiting for the right moment. Another, more exciting, kind of photograph happens when unpredictable events — a torrential thunderstorm, an ephemeral rainbow or a rare snowfall — occur when I'm lucky enough to be in the wilderness. At these times, which are incredibly fleeting, I try to contain my excitement and work as quickly as I can to capture the image. These sometimes-crazed shooting sessions are, for me, the most intoxicating and rewarding work I do.

Thor's Hammer oversees a wintery sunrise,
Bryce Canyon National Park

*Snowy sunset illuminates Zion Canyon Overlook,
Zion National Park*

*Sunset washes sandstone butte before a distant
Needles District, Canyonlands National Park*

" . . . minute by minute the horizon's darkness defined itself
as the blue-domed shadow of the earth cast on the sky,
thinning at its upward arc to violet, lavender, pale lilac, but
clearly defined, steadily darkening upward until it swallowed
all the sky's light and the stars pierced through it."

Heavy snow caps Bryce Amphitheater,
Bryce Canyon National Park

Flashflood waterfall follows September thunderstorm,
Seven-Mile Creek

Overleaf: *Rainbow soars over Balanced Rock,*
Arches National Park

"In the canyons you do not have the sweep of sky, the long
views, the freedom of movement on foot, but you do have
the protection of cliffs, the secret places, cool water, arches
and bridges and caves, and the sunken canyon stillness into
which, musical as water falling into a plunge pool, the
canyon wrens pour their showers of notes in the mornings."

Clearing storm reveals snow-dusted
Mount Timpanogos, Alpine Loop

Wintery sunset gilds Utah Lake, Utah Lake State Park

". . . the importance of the mountains as watersheds, as the
mothers of streams, cannot be overstated. . . . Both surface
streams and the underground water table for
hundreds of miles depend upon the fact that water is not
only caught by the mountains but stored there."

Shades of sunset on the Great Salt Lake,
Great Salt Lake State Park

Snowy sunrise above the Colorado River,
Dead Horse Point State Park

Overleaf: *Morning stormlight washes the Maze*
Overlook, Canyonlands National Park

"Every night we watched the earth-shadow climb the hollow
sky, and every dawn we watched the same blue shadow sink
down . . . to disappear at the instant when the sun splintered
sparks off the rim."

MOTION

Still images can be amazingly effective in portraying the beauty of motion. As photographers struggle to reduce the three-dimensional world to a small piece of one-dimensional plastic, they also work to distill movement, or the idea of movement, from the natural scene. Motion can appear in still images as a blur or as a progression of powerful shapes and forms that produces the feeling of movement.

Water, the great shaper of the Utah landscape, is the most apparent moving force in my photographs. The milky appearance of flowing water is caused by the long film exposures necessary for a large-format camera. While photographing the violent denouement of a flash flood on a dark summer evening, I was forced to expose the churning waters for 30 seconds as they sped past me toward the Colorado River. Clouds, too, although not usually moving fast enough to blur, can be as turbulent and suggestive of motion as rivers or streams.

Morning light on Lower Calf Creek Falls,
near the Escalante River

Overleaf: *Clearing winter storm,*
Cedar Breaks National Monument

Icy waterfall plunges into Price Canyon,
Wasatch Plateau

Paintbrush wildflowers bloom beside a rocky cascade,
Spanish Valley

"All I knew was that it was pure delight to be where
the land lifted in peaks and plunged in canyons, and to sniff
air thin, spray-cooled, full of pine and spruce smells,
and to be so close-seeming to the improbable indigo sky."

Falls soak cave in the Wasatch Range,
Wasatch National Forest

Diminutive cascade feeds the Virgin River in
Zion Narrows, Zion National Park

"Often these canyons, pursued upward, ended in falls, and
sometimes the falls came down through a slot or a skylight
in the roof of a domed chamber, to trickle down the wall
into a plunge pool that made a lyrical dunk bath on a hot
day. In such chambers the light was dim, reflected,
richly colored."

*Spring runoff replenishes falls in Coyote Gulch,
Glen Canyon National Recreation Area*

Storm waves on a cloudy afternoon, Great Salt Lake

*Overleaf: Waterfall washes over lava rock in
Great West Canyon, Zion National Park*

"I gave my heart to the mountains the minute I stood beside
this river with its spray in my face and watched it thunder
into foam, smooth to green glass over sunken rocks, shatter
to foam again. I was fascinated by how it sped by and yet
was always there; its roar shook both the earth and me."

Winter storm over Junction Butte,
Canyonlands National Park

Narrow stream channel cuts through Great West
Canyon, Zion National Park

". . . we feel descending on us, as gentle as evening on a
blazing day, the remembered canyon silence. It is a stillness
like no other I have experienced, for at the very instant of
bouncing and echoing every slight noise off cliffs and around
bends, the canyons swallow them."

PLACE

One easy lesson about the Utah wilderness is that a visit to a new place always exceeds expectations. There is always more to see, more to find and more to experience than the imagination can conceive. My first trip through Cataract Canyon in Canyonlands National Park many years ago taught me that well. I was not prepared for the ferocity of the rapids, the depth and rugged beauty of the canyon walls or the whimsical charm of the Dolls House above Spanish Bottom. No matter how many places I explore, it seems there is always word of a wonderful new rock art panel to see or a huge new arch to photograph. Often I am reminded of the motto of a Moab tour company from a few years back: "Nobody's seen it all; it's just too big."

Water trickles through the Subway in
Great West Canyon, Zion National Park

Winter sunrise on Stansbury Island, Great Salt Lake

Summer sunrise reflection of Ostler Peak,
High Uintas Wilderness

Overleaf: *Aftermath of a winter storm, Book Cliffs*

". . . one experiences the western *feel* — a dryness in the
nostrils, a cracking of the lips, a transparent crystalline
quality of the light . . . a new palette of gray, sage-green,
sulphur yellow, buff, toned white, rust red, a new flora and
fauna, a new ecology."

Morning light on autumn-tinged maples and aspen,
Mount Timpanogos Wilderness

Vestiges of winter on Twin Peaks, Mount Olympus Wilderness

"The sun comes fairly late over the walls of the canyon, and before
sunrise the valley lies in a clear gray light so transparent that every leaf
on the river cottonwoods is distinct, the timbered hillsides are
sharp-edged and shadowless. The wind has not yet begun to stir."

*Snow-dusted San Juan River Canyon,
San Juan Goosenecks State Park*

Leaf-strewn miner's cabin, Ophir

Overleaf: *Sculpted Navajo sandstone swirls up from
the Green River, Labyrinth Canyon
Wilderness Study Area*

"[Man's] confrontations are therefore likely to be with
landscape, which seems to define the West and its meaning
better than any of its forming cultures, and with himself in
the context of that landscape."

Prickly-pear cactus blooms beneath a morning sun,
Great Salt Lake

Narrow canyon near the Escalante River,
Scorpion Canyon Wilderness Study Area

"In that country you cannot raise your eyes — unless you're
in a canyon — without looking a hundred miles. You can
hear coyotes. . . . You can see in every sandy pocket the pug
tracks of wildcats . . ."

MICROCOSM

Since the time of the great frontier photographer William Henry Jackson, Utah's mountains and deserts have lent themselves to the "big landscape," photographs of the majesty on the horizon. While continuing to photograph the grandeur of infinity, I always feel the desire to photograph the minutiae that most people overlook. Sometimes there is more joy in bringing to a viewer's attention a small, neglected marvel than the universally recognized beauty of a major tourist attraction. The idyllic canyons of southern Utah brim with possibilities: the abstractions of erosion on a tapestried rock wall or the intoxicating beauty of a moist wall of monkeyflowers and columbine. As I work with a big camera and small subjects, passersby sometimes ask, "What are you photographing?" I know when I hear that question that I may be on to something good — something beautiful others have ignored.

Fallen leaves in a natural oil seep,
Negro Bill Canyon Wilderness Study Area

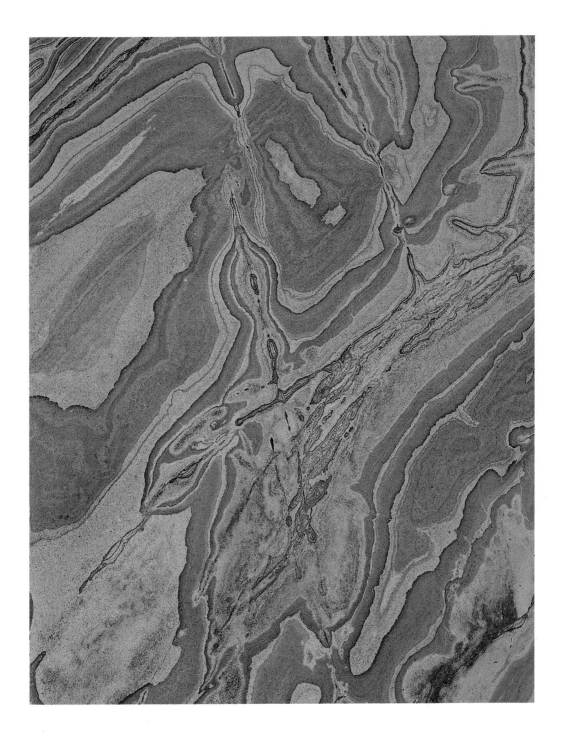

Patterns in banded rhyolite, near Saint George

Death brings beauty to conifer branches, High Uintas Wilderness

Overleaf: *Reeds at sunset along the Colorado River, Grand County*

"[The wilderness] is good for us when we are young, because of the incomparable sanity it can bring briefly, as vacation and rest, into our insane lives. It is important to us when we are old simply because it is there — important, that is, simply as idea."

Sandstone patterns in Johnson Canyon along the Arizona Strip, Utah/Arizona border

Shore rocks at Promontory Point, Great Salt Lake

"I want to speak for the wilderness idea as something that has helped form our character and that has certainly shaped our history as a people. . . . Something will have gone out of us as a people if we ever let the remaining wilderness be destroyed. . . ."

Erosion's handiwork at the Dolls House,
Maze District, Canyonlands National Park

Reflections near the San Juan River,
Slickhorn Canyon Wilderness Study Area

"We need wilderness preserved — as much of it as is still
left, and as many kinds — because it was the challenge
against which our character as a people was formed."

THE ANCIENTS

Utah's archeological heritage has diminished greatly over just the few years I have been photographing the enthralling ruins and rock art of our state. Many rock art panels have been vandalized and some have been almost completely destroyed. Small Anasazi towns that stood intact through centuries of frying heat, winter blizzard and autumn monsoon have fallen victim to the greed of pot hunters. Even nature herself dealt a blow when a flash flood destroyed part of a magnificent panel in Canyonlands National Park. Although I feel fortunate to have preserved on film some of what has been lost, it is small consolation.
If you happen upon any of the ruins, pictographs or petroglyphs pictured here, please treat them with the respect due the enchanting civilization that created them. And, if we are to have any legacy for our children and grandchildren, we must do more to protect these magical places.

Sunbeamed interior of an Anasazi Indian ceremonial kiva, unnamed Wilderness Study Area

*The Harvest Scene, a pictograph panel
in the Maze District, Canyonlands National Park*

*Last light of day warms a ruin,
Canyonlands National Park*

"I want a foot on earth, I am forced to believe in human
community and in Time. I believe we are Time's prisoners,
I believe Time is our safety and our strength."

Petroglyphs at Island Park on the Green River,
Dinosaur National Monument

The Green Mask pictograph presides over Grand
Gulch, Grand Gulch Primitive Area

"And the entire history of the West, when we hold at arm's
length the excitement, adventure, romance, and legendry, is
a history of resources often mismanaged and of constraining
conditions often misunderstood or disregarded. Here, as
elsewhere, settlement went by trial and error; only here the
trials were sometimes terrible for those who suffered them,
and the errors did permanent injury to the land."

Monster petroglyphs in the San Rafael Swell,
near Ferron

Ruin of an Anasazi turkey pen,
Grand Gulch Primitive Area

"... the West ... is the native home of hope. When it fully
learns that cooperation, not rugged individualism, is the
pattern that most characterizes and preserves it, then it will
have achieved itself and outlived its origins. Then it has a
chance to create a society to match its scenery."

TECHNICAL
INFORMATION

All photographs in this book were made with a 4x5 Toyo field camera on 4x5 Ektachrome 64, 100 and 100 plus and Fujichrome 50 and 100 films. Lens focal lengths were 65mm, 75mm, 90mm, 135mm, 210mm, 300mm, 360mm, 400mm and 500mm. Warming filters (81A and 81B) were used at times with the Ektachrome films, while no filtration was used with the Fujichrome. In every case, an attempt was made to match the printed image with the original transparency. Photographs were not "boosted" in the printing process to enhance color.

Acknowledgements

Heartfelt thanks to my Moab family, Jim and Peggy Nissen, Donna and Steve Brownell, Glen Lathrop, Steve Mulligan and Vicki Gigliotti, Mike Hill, Barry Miller and Karla Vanderzaden, and Bruce Hucko for their continual support and encouragement. Also thanks to Ken Sanders and Debby Berdan in Salt Lake City and to Matt Gigliotti in Colorado Springs. My wife and children especially have my gratitude and love for their patience and understanding during my sometimes lengthy absences.

Moonrise at Delicate Arch, Arches National Park